Let Freedom Ring

The United States Constitution

by Kristal Leebrick

Consultant:
Terry L. Jordan, Author
The U.S. Constitution and Fascinating Facts about It

Bridgestone Books
an imprint of Capstone Press
Mankato, Minnesota

Bridgestone Books are published by Capstone Press,
1710 Roe Crest Drive, North Mankato, Minnesota 56003.
www.capstonepub.com

 Books published by Capstone Press are manufactured with paper containing at least 10 percent post-consumer waste.

Library of Congress Cataloging-in-Publication Data
Leebrick, Kristal, 1958–
    The United States Constitution / by Kristal Leebrick.
        p. cm. — (Let freedom ring)
    Includes bibliographical references and index.
    ISBN-13: 978-0-7368-1094-4 (hardcover)
    ISBN-10: 0-7368-1094-3 (hardcover)
    ISBN-13: 978-0-7368-4495-6 (softcover pbk.)
    ISBN-10: 0-7368-4495-3 (softcover pbk.)
    1. Constitutional history—United States—Juvenile literature. [1. Constitutional history.] I. Title. II. Series.
    KF4541 .Z9 L44 2002
    342.73′029—dc21   2001003229
                                                                                                    CIP

Summary: Discusses how and why the United States Constitution was created; includes the difficulties with ratification by the states; and explains the Bill of Rights.

Editorial Credits
Rebecca Aldridge, editor; Kia Bielke, cover designer, interior layout designer, and interior illustrator; Jennifer Schonborn, cover production designer; Deirdre Barton, photo researcher

Photo Credits
Cover: Howard Chandler Christy/US Capitol Historical Society (large); Joseph Sohm; Visions of America/CORBIS (small); Stock Montage, Inc., 5, 9, 11, 19, 33; Hulton/Archive Photos, 6, 31, 37; Reunion des Musees Nationaux/Art Resource, NY, 13; Library of Congress, 15, 43 (small); PhotoSphere, 17, 43 (left); CORBIS, 23; The Pierpont Morgan Library/Art Resource, NY, 25; Joseph Sohm; Visions of America/CORBIS, 26; Unicorn Stock Photos/Joe Sohm, 27; C.P. George/Visuals Unlimited, 28; Bettmann/CORBIS, 34, 41; Jacques M. Chenet/CORBIS, 38

Printed in the United States of America in North Mankato, Minnesota.
042013   007255R

Table of Contents

Chapter One

A Nation of 13 States

During the Revolutionary War (1775–1783), the 13 colonies joined together to fight against Britain for independence. However, after the war's end, people living in the former colonies did not think of the United States as a nation. Each state was sovereign, meaning it was its own boss. Every person was a citizen of his or her state. It was as if each state were its own country. Now, instead of paying taxes to Britain, Americans paid taxes to the sovereign state in which they lived.

The states were part of what people called a confederation, a voluntary league of states. Each state had its own government, but every state also sent representatives to a congress. The Congress made decisions about matters of common concern to all states.

The Revolutionary War lasted from 1775 to 1783. After the war's end, Britain recognized the United States as a free and independent nation.

A Weak Central Government

In 1777, the Congress had written the Articles of Confederation, which set rules for a federal, or central, government. Their experience under British rule made the citizens of the United States careful. They did not want to give a central government too much power.

The government formed by the Articles of Confederation loosely held the states together in a league of friendship. Each state agreed to work with the national government.

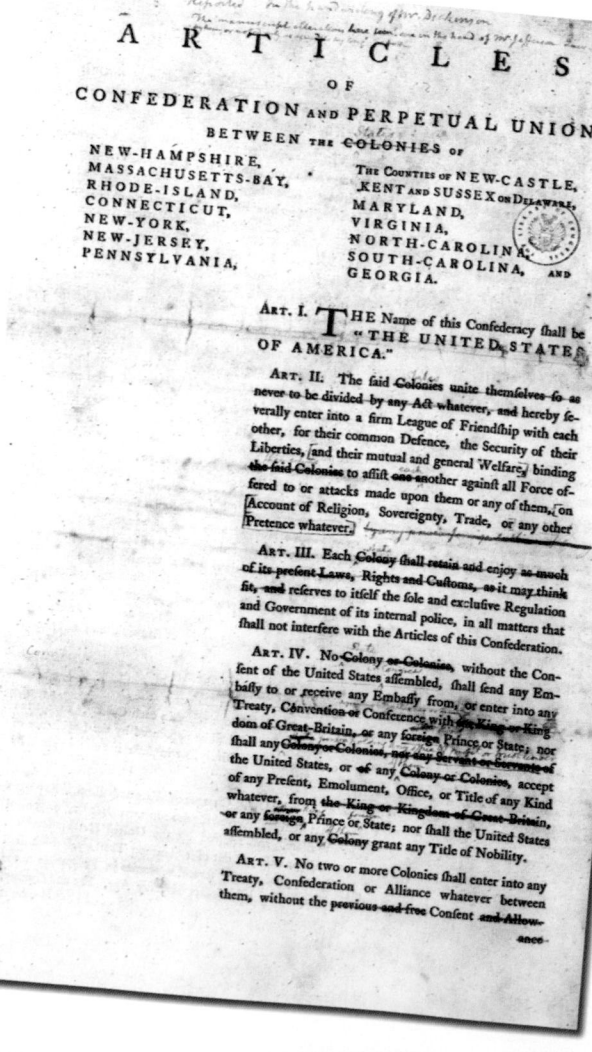

Quote

Here is how George Washington described the government under the Articles of Confederation: "a half-starved limping government, that appears to be always moving upon crutches and tottering at every step."

However, the government formed by the Articles of Confederation had almost no power. Under the Articles of Confederation, the government could not raise money with taxes. It could not make trade agreements with other countries; each state made its own. The government could not create an army or a navy, which soon became a problem.

Plenty of Problems

After 1783, Spain owned Florida and other southern areas, including the city of New Orleans. Spain would not let the states ship goods down the Mississippi River and through New Orleans.

Britain was not honoring the Treaty of Paris, the agreement signed at the end of the American

Money Troubles

Taxes were not the only money problems in the states. Costs were rising. For example, a pound (.45 kilograms) of tea could cost as much as $100.

Revolutionary War. The British refused to leave fur-trading posts in New York. The United States had no army to deal with Spain. Without an army, the country could not force Britain to honor the promises it had made.

Financial troubles hit the sovereign states. The federal government owed money to other countries that had helped them in the war. The people owed money to their state governments. Some states printed paper money, but it was worthless. This money could not be used in other states. Some states used British pounds, while other states used Spanish dollars.

After the war, the financial problems that troubled all the states hit farmers especially hard. The Massachusetts government made the matter worse by placing heavy taxes on farmland. Then the government demanded that these taxes be paid in cash. Debt was considered a crime, and those who could not pay were thrown into debtor's prison.

From 1786 to 1787, Daniel Shays led a militant protest against heavy taxes in Massachusetts. His men were ready to fight. Their protest became known as Shays' Rebellion. The Articles of Confederation were not working, and there was no authority to make them work.

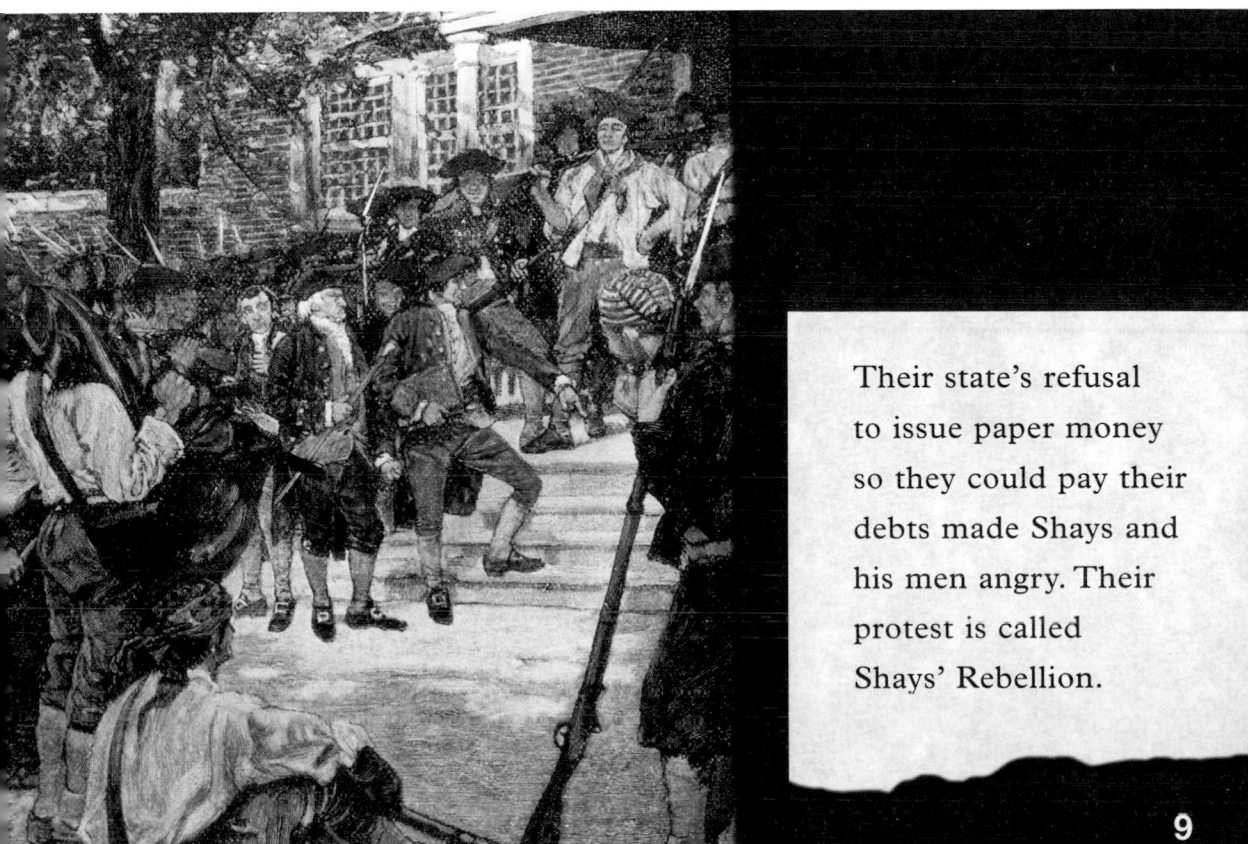

Their state's refusal to issue paper money so they could pay their debts made Shays and his men angry. Their protest is called Shays' Rebellion.

Debtor's Prisons

Timothy Bigelow had been an officer in the Continental Army during the Revolutionary War. After the war, he returned to his home in Massachusetts and struggled to continue his blacksmith business. Unfortunately, he owed so much money that he was thrown into a debtor's prison. This was a place where people were held until someone paid their debt or taxes for them. No one paid Bigelow's debt, and he remained in debtor's prison until he became ill and died.

In the late 1700s, Isaiah Thomas, a Massachusetts newspaperman, brought attention to Bigelow's story. He thought it showed why poor conditions in debtor's prisons needed to change.

A Fix Is Needed

Many of the men who had led the fight against the British years earlier were worried about the United States. These American men knew that the states could not be truly independent of each other and survive. Already, the states were arguing about the borders between them. These particular American men thought the country would fall apart if it did not have a powerful central government that could act for all the states. Even the British did not think the new country would last.

Alexander Hamilton made a suggestion to the Congress. He thought that a Grand Convention or Federal Convention should be held in Philadelphia. The purpose of this large gathering of people would be to improve the existing government. The Congress agreed, and a date was set for the meeting—May 14, 1787.

Alexander Hamilton had helped in the fight against the British. He thought that a meeting was needed to discuss improving the United States government.

Chapter Two

Summer in Philadelphia

The first to arrive in Philadelphia for the convention in the spring of 1787 was 36-year-old James Madison. This Virginia representative came early and eagerly. He had studied hard and read about the governments of ancient Greece and Rome as well as those of other places and times. Madison brought what he had learned to the convention.

All the states except Rhode Island sent delegates to the convention. Rhode Island would have nothing to do with it. Neither would Patrick Henry, the governor of Virginia. In reference to the meeting, he said, "I smelt a rat." Henry thought the convention was a plot to take away the rights of the individual states.

The Convention Begins

Finally, on May 25, enough delegates had arrived to begin the convention. As soon as the meeting began, Robert Morris of Philadelphia

James Madison is now known as the "Father of the Constitution." People said he was the best-prepared delegate at the Constitutional Convention in 1787.

Need a Lift?

Benjamin Franklin of Pennsylvania made the showiest entrance to the convention. He entered the hall on a richly decorated sedan chair that was attached to four long poles. Four prisoners from the Philadelphia Jail carried him in this chair. Franklin suffered from the pains of gout and old age. Gout is a disease that can cause joints to swell and become painful. This chair, from Paris, France, allowed Franklin to be moved without being shaken about.

moved to elect Revolutionary War hero George Washington of Virginia as the convention president. Not one delegate voted against Washington.

The election of Washington as the convention's leader was an important event. It helped secure the convention's success because the people of America trusted him.

James Madison asked that he be allowed to take notes during the entire convention. He sat in the front of the room near Washington's desk. Throughout the summer, Madison kept an account of the arguments, motions, and votes. Others took notes at the convention, too. But it is said that Madison's notes were the most thorough and exact.

Secrecy and Quiet

One of the first things the delegates voted on at the convention was secrecy. Despite the hot summer weather, they agreed to keep the windows of the building closed. Guards were posted in front of the State House (now called Independence Hall).

The delegates needed to shut out noise from outside so they could concentrate. They convinced

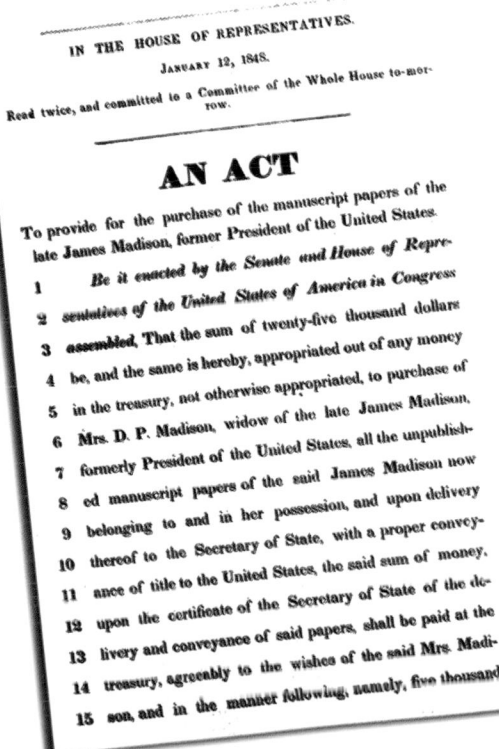

In 1837, President Andrew Jackson asked Congress to pay $30,000 for the journal with Madison's convention notes, so they could be published. In 1848, Congress provided an additional $25,000 to buy Madison's remaining papers from his wife. The act proposing the 1848 purchase appears at left.

Who's Who at the Convention

A total of 55 men attended the convention, although not everyone was there at the same time. Most of the men were wealthy property owners. Some were lawyers, planters, teachers, ministers, doctors, or merchants. No women and no people of color attended.

No rules were set for how to pick delegates to attend the Convention. There also were no limits on how many men could attend. Each state government chose its own delegates. Most of these men knew each other before the meeting began. They had fought together in the American Revolution or worked together in the Continental Congress.

the city to cover the cobblestone streets around the State House with straw and dirt. This covering softened the sounds of horses' hooves and wagon wheels as they clattered down the streets.

The delegates agreed that nothing spoken inside the State House would be printed in the newspapers. They agreed not to talk about their discussions outside the building. Several delegates planned to stick by Benjamin Franklin's side throughout the convention. He was known as someone who loved to talk a little too much at parties. The delegates feared he might speak and let details about the meetings slip.

Finally, it was time for the convention delegates to answer the question that Franklin asked: Do we have the wisdom to govern ourselves?

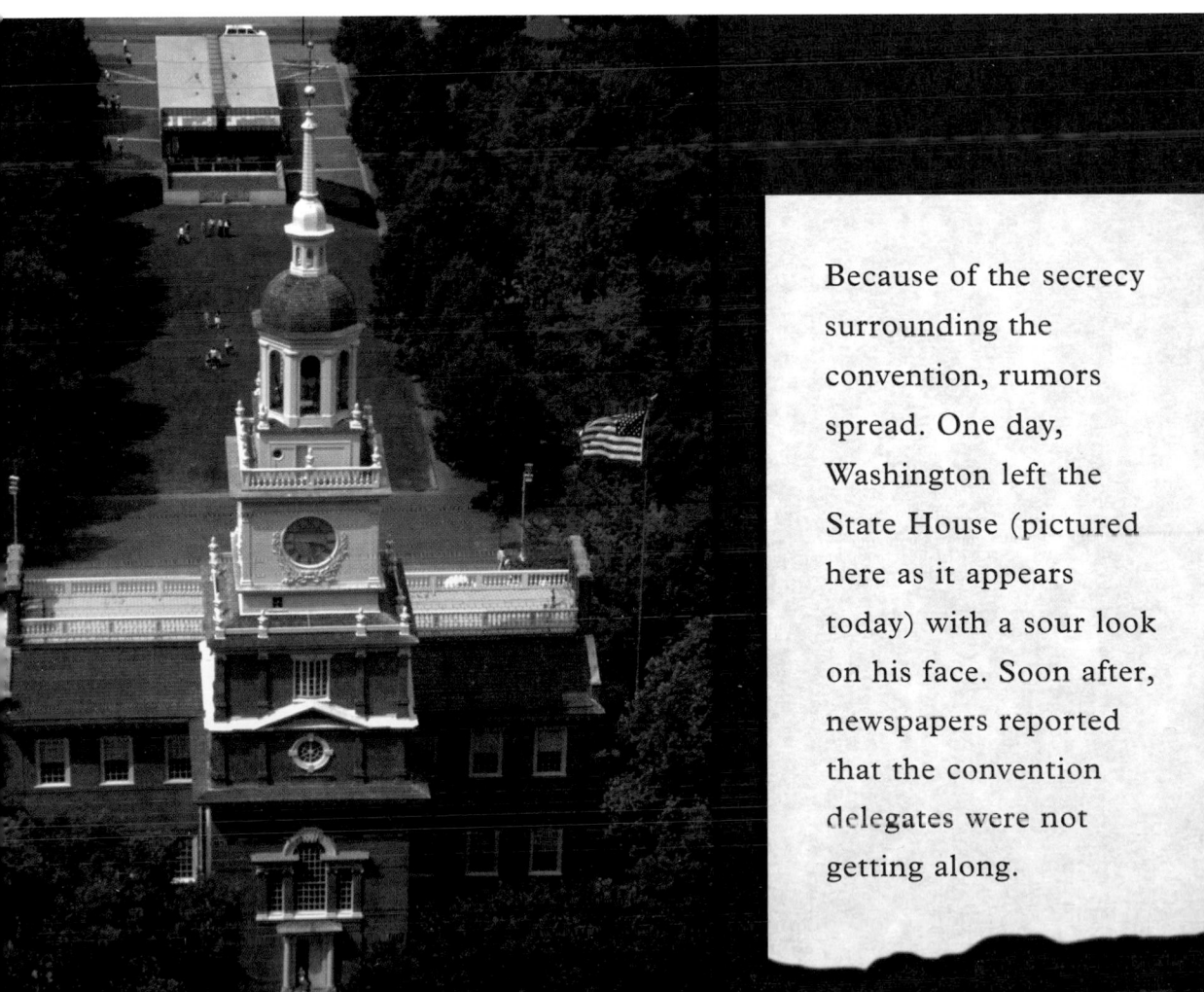

Because of the secrecy surrounding the convention, rumors spread. One day, Washington left the State House (pictured here as it appears today) with a sour look on his face. Soon after, newspapers reported that the convention delegates were not getting along.

Chapter Three

Forming a More Perfect Union

The original purpose of the Grand Convention was to adjust the Articles of Confederation. It soon became clear, however, that the delegates needed to develop a completely different style of government.

The delegates set out to write an entirely new document creating a new national government. After a week of debate, the delegates decided on a government with three branches, much like their state governments. The legislative branch would make laws. The executive branch would put the laws into effect and make sure they were followed. The judiciary branch would settle disagreements that arose under the laws.

The Virginia Plan

Edmund Randolph of Virginia presented a plan written by James Madison. This Virginia Plan called for the three-branch system of government and a two-house legislature.

THE FOUNDATION OF AMERICAN GOVERNMENT

The Grand Convention is now known as the Constitutional
Convention because the delegates there created the
Constitution of the United States.

The United States in 1787

Virginia was the biggest of the 13 states in both size and population, so the plan also was called the large-state plan. It gave larger states greater control in the legislative branch by giving states with a larger population more delegates in the Congress.

The New Jersey Plan

The small states submitted their own plan drawn up by William Paterson of New Jersey. The New Jersey Plan called for a one-house legislature similar to the one under the Articles of Confederation. People referred to the New Jersey Plan as the small-state plan. It called for equal representation, with each state having only one vote.

These two plans set off heated debates. Seven states voted against the New Jersey Plan. When the Virginia Plan came up for a vote, the small states joined together to defeat it. Delegates formed a committee to work out a compromise.

The Great Compromise

The work by this small group of men is now known as the Great Compromise. They proposed that the government's legislative branch have two houses: the

House of Representatives and the Senate.

The members of the House of Representatives would be chosen according to each state's population. The states with more people would have more representatives. This pleased those members who supported the Virginia Plan.

The Senate would have one representative from each state, regardless of the state's population. (Later, this number changed to two representatives.) This idea pleased those who supported the New Jersey Plan.

After the compromise, the convention delegates chose a committee to put the new constitution in order. While the committee worked, the rest of the delegates took a 10-day vacation.

Free Time

During their free time, some delegates had pictures of themselves made with a special machine. It copied the exact silhouette (shadow) of a person's facial features. The machine captured people's images 50 years before the invention of the photograph. Madison, Franklin, and Washington all had silhouettes made of themselves.

The Three-Fifths Compromise

Southern delegates wanted slaves to be counted as part of a state's population. The northern states protested. Slaves made up almost 20 percent of the nation's population in the late 1700s, and most lived in the South. Counting slaves would increase the number of southern seats in the House of Representatives. This method of counting would give the South control of the House.

The delegates compromised. They allowed a slave to count as three-fifths of a free person when state populations were counted. The compromise meant that three out of every five slaves would be counted in this census for the purposes of taxation and representation. This agreement was called the Three-Fifths Compromise.

Chapter Four

We the People

The Constitution provided for a federal system in which power would be divided between states and a central government. The delegates felt strongly that it was dangerous for any branch of government to have too much power.

The delegates were careful to build a set of checks and balances into the Constitution. For example, a majority in both the Senate and the House of Representatives has to agree on a proposed law. Yet the president of the United States can veto, or reject, it. But Congress can override, or undo, the veto with a two-thirds majority vote in each house of Congress.

Individual Rights

When the final version of the Constitution was presented to the delegates, some had second thoughts. Many delegates still were not pleased with

The delegates gathered back together on August 6, 1787. Even into September, they worked to bring the document to its final form.

Handwriting the Constitution

Jacob Shallus did the handwriting for the Constitution. He was a clerk at the Pennsylvania State Assembly (government). His office was in the same building where the Constitutional Convention took place. Jacob received $30 for his work on the Constitution.

the document. One argument was that there was no bill of rights. Many states had a bill of rights written into their constitutions. These individual rights included freedom of religion, freedom of speech, and the right to a trial by jury.

Supporters of the Constitution said there was no need for a bill of rights. Individuals would keep all the rights guaranteed, or secured, in their state constitutions. This, they said, was taken for granted.

On September 17, four months after the convention began, the delegates signed the finished Constitution. Benjamin Franklin needed help signing because of his age. Franklin cried as he signed the document because he was overcome with emotion.

Three delegates backed out of signing the Constitution. Edmund Randolph wanted to see

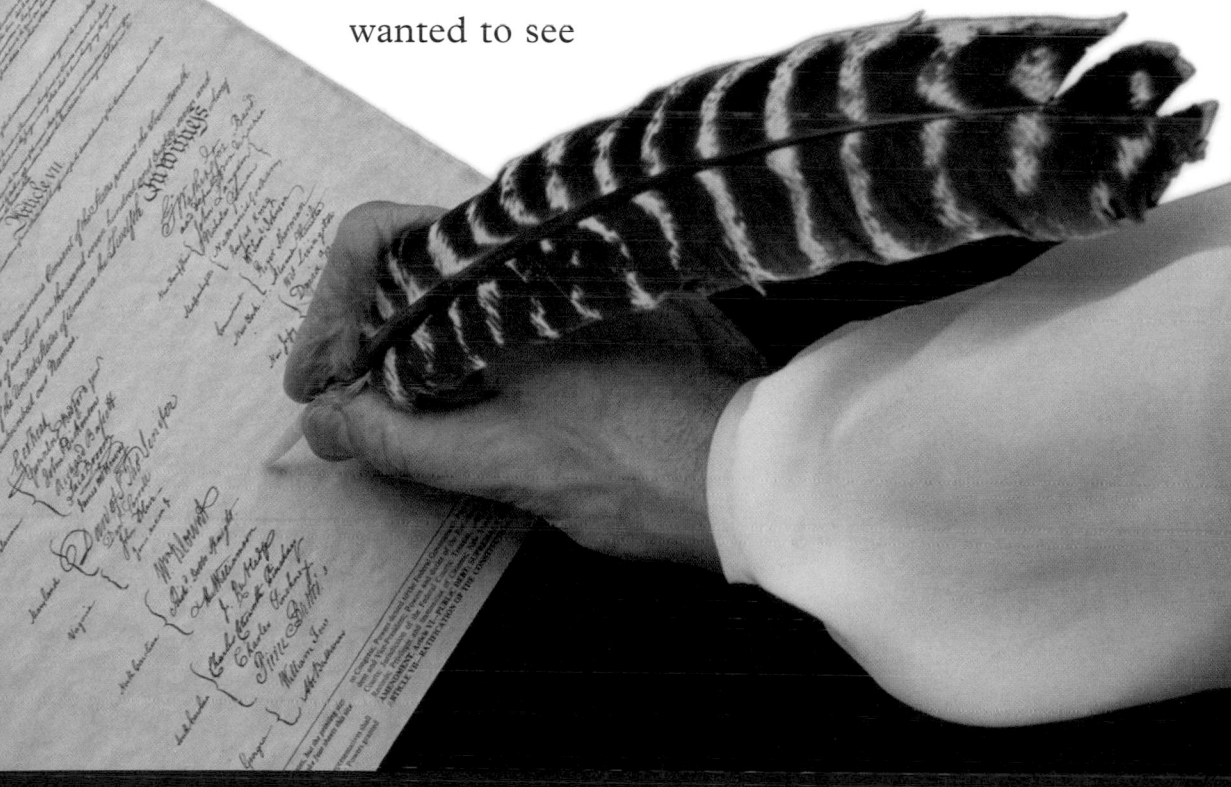

Thirty-nine of the remaining 42 delegates at the convention signed the Constitution.

how the country reacted before he made up his mind. George Mason of Virginia said he could not sign the document without a bill of rights. Elbridge Gerry of Massachusetts also refused to sign.

Those who did sign did not necessarily feel the Constitution was perfect. However, they did feel that it was something a majority of people could accept. Now, it was time to show the Constitution to the rest of the country.

This is the room in the Philadelphia State House where the delegates adopted and signed the Constitution.

An Outline of the Constitution

The Constitution of the United States is made up of the preamble and seven articles. A basic description of the preamble and each article follows.

Preamble: Makes a promise to the people of the United States; The people can expect the government to protect them from other countries and to provide peace, justice, and safety at home.

Article 1: Outlines the legislative branch; It gives all lawmaking powers to the U.S. Congress. Congress also collects taxes, borrows money, regulates foreign trade, sets rules for citizenship, and declares war.

Article 2: Outlines the executive branch, or the U.S. presidency; The president can make treaties with and appoint ambassadors to other countries. He or she can appoint Supreme Court judges with approval from Congress. The president is the head of the military.

Article 3: Describes the judicial branch, or U.S. Supreme Court; The Supreme Court decides if laws are Constitutional and reviews decisions of lower courts.

Article 4: Says that the rights a citizen has in one state will be respected in all states

Article 5: Allows Congress to amend, or change, the Constitution

Article 6: Declares that the Constitution is the supreme, or highest, law of the land

Article 7: Tells how the Constitution would be ratified, or approved, which it was in 1788

Chapter Five

Selling the Constitution

Soon, citizens throughout the 13 states had an opportunity to see the Constitution. People were quick to take sides. Those who were for the Constitution called themselves Federalists. People against it called themselves Anti-Federalists. They were in the majority. These people feared centralized national power. To them, the Constitution seemed to outline a government too much like the British government they had just fought against.

Alexander Hamilton, James Madison, and John Jay were three strong Federalists. They began writing newspaper articles explaining just how the new Constitution would work. They did this to try to change the minds of Anti-Federalists in New York.

These articles, or essays, were put together in book form and called the *Federalist Papers*. They circulated throughout the United States. In the

The Pennsylvania Packet, *and Daily Advertiser.*

[Price Four-Pence.] WEDNESDAY, September 19, 1787. [No. 2690.]

WE, the People of the United States, in order to form a more perfect Union, establish Justice, insure domestic Tranquility, provide for the common Defence, promote the General Welfare, and secure the Blessings of Liberty to Ourselves and our Posterity, do ordain and establish this Constitution for the United States of America.

ARTICLE I.

Sect. 1. ALL legislative powers herein granted shall be vested in a Congress of the United States, which shall consist of a Senate and House of Representatives.

Sect. 2. The House of Representatives shall be composed of members chosen every second year by the people of the several states, and the electors in each state shall have the qualifications requisite for electors of the most numerous branch of the state legislature.

No person shall be a representative who shall not have attained to the age of twenty-five years, and been seven years a citizen of the United States, and who shall not, when elected, be an inhabitant of that state in which he shall be chosen.

Representatives and direct taxes shall be apportioned among the several states which may be included within this Union, according to their respective numbers, which shall be determined by adding to the whole number of free persons, including those bound to service for a term of years, and excluding Indians not taxed, three-fifths of all other persons. The actual enumeration shall be made within three years after the first meeting of the Congress of the United States, and within every subsequent term of ten years, in such manner as they shall by law direct. The number of representatives shall not exceed one for every thirty thousand, but each state shall have at least one representative; and until such enumeration shall be made, the state of New-Hampshire shall be entitled to chuse three, Massachusetts eight, Rhode-Island and Providence Plantations one, Connecticut five, New-York six, New-Jersey four, Pennsylvania eight, Delaware one, Maryland six, Virginia ten, North-Carolina five, South-Carolina five, and Georgia three.

When vacancies happen in the representation from any state, the Executive authority thereof shall issue writs of election to fill such vacancies.

The House of Representatives shall chuse their Speaker and other officers; and shall have the sole power of impeachment.

Sect. 3. The Senate of the United States shall be composed of two senators from each state, chosen by the legislature thereof, for six years; and each senator shall have one vote.

Immediately after they shall be assembled in consequence of the first election, they shall be divided as equally as may be into three classes. The seats of the senators of the first class shall be vacated at the expiration of the second year, of the second class at the expiration of the fourth year, and of the third class at the expiration of the sixth year, so that one-third may be chosen every second year; and if vacancies happen by resignation, or otherwise, during the recess of the Legislature of any state, the Executive thereof may make temporary appointments until the next meeting of the Legislature, which shall then fill such vacancies.

No person shall be a senator who shall not have attained to the age of thirty years, and been nine years a citizen of the United States, and who shall not, when elected, be an inhabitant of that state for which he shall be chosen.

The Vice-President of the United States shall be President of the senate, but shall have no vote, unless they be equally divided.

The Senate shall chuse their other officers, and also a President pro tempore, in the absence of the Vice-President, or when he shall exercise the office of President of the United States.

The Senate shall have the sole power to try all impeachments. When sitting for that purpose, they shall be on oath or affirmation. When the President of the United States is tried, the Chief Justice shall preside: And no person shall be convicted without the concurrence of two-thirds of the members present.

Judgment in cases of impeachment shall not extend further than to removal from office, and disqualification to hold and enjoy any office of honor, trust or profit under the United States; but the party convicted shall nevertheless be liable and subject to indictment, trial, judgment and punishment, according to law.

Sect. 4. The times, places and manner of holding elections for senators and representatives, shall be prescribed in each state by the legislature thereof; but the Congress may at any time by law make or alter such regulations, except as to the places of chusing Senators.

The Congress shall assemble at least once in every year, and such meeting shall be on the first Monday in December, unless they shall by law appoint a different day.

Sect. 5. Each house shall be the judge of the elections, returns and qualifications of its own members, and a majority of each shall constitute a quorum to do business; but a smaller number may adjourn from day to day, and may be authorised to compel the attendance of absent members, in such manner, and under such penalties as each house may provide.

Each house may determine the rules of its proceedings, punish its members for disorderly behaviour, and, with the concurrence of two-thirds, expel a member.

Each house shall keep a journal of its proceedings, and from time to time publish the same, excepting such parts as may in their judgment require secrecy; and the yeas and nays of the members of either house on any question shall, at the desire of one-fifth of those present, be entered on the journal.

Neither house, during the session of Congress, shall, without the consent of the other, adjourn for more than three days, nor to any other place than that in which the two houses shall be sitting.

Sect. 6. The senators and representatives shall receive a compensation for their services, to be ascertained by law, and paid out of the treasury of the United States. They shall in all cases, except treason, felony and breach of the peace, be privileged from arrest during their attendance at the session of their respective houses, and in going to and returning from the same; and for any speech or debate in either house, they shall not be questioned in any other place.

No senator or representative shall, during the time for which he was elected, be appointed to any civil office under the authority of the United States, which shall have been created, or the emoluments whereof shall have been encreased during such time; and no person holding any office under the United States, shall be a member of either house during his continuance in office.

Sect. 7. All bills for raising revenue shall originate in the house of representatives; but the senate may propose or concur with amendments as on other bills.

Every bill which shall have passed the house of representatives and the senate, shall, before it become a law, be presented to the president of the United States; if he approve he shall sign it, but if not he shall return it, with his objections to that house in which it shall have originated, who shall enter the objections at large on their journal, and proceed to reconsider it. If after such reconsideration two-thirds of that house shall agree to pass the bill, it shall be sent, together with the objections, to the other house, by which it shall likewise be reconsidered, and if approved by two-thirds of that house, it shall become a law. But in all such cases the votes of both houses shall

---

Two days after the Constitutional Convention ended, the Constitution appeared in newspapers like this one throughout the city of Philadelphia.

A Change of Heart

Rhode Island did not even send a delegate to the Pennsylvania convention in 1787. However, even that state ratified the Constitution. Rhode Island came into the Union in May 1790—a year after George Washington became president of the United States.

end, the Constitution may not have been approved without these writings.

Debates for Ratification

The states held conventions and debated the Constitution. They then voted on whether to ratify it. This process took more than six months. The biggest stumbling block was the lack of a bill of rights. People were concerned about their individual freedoms.

The Federalists tried to reassure people. They said that the Constitution could easily be amended to include those rights. However, a government had to be formed first.

The delegates at the Constitutional Convention had agreed that nine of the 13 states needed to approve the Constitution. Only then could it become the law of the land. Delaware was the first to ratify the Constitution on December 7, 1787. On June 21, 1788, New Hampshire became the ninth state to ratify it. With that vote, the United States of America officially became one nation. Eventually, all the states ratified the Constitution and joined the Union.

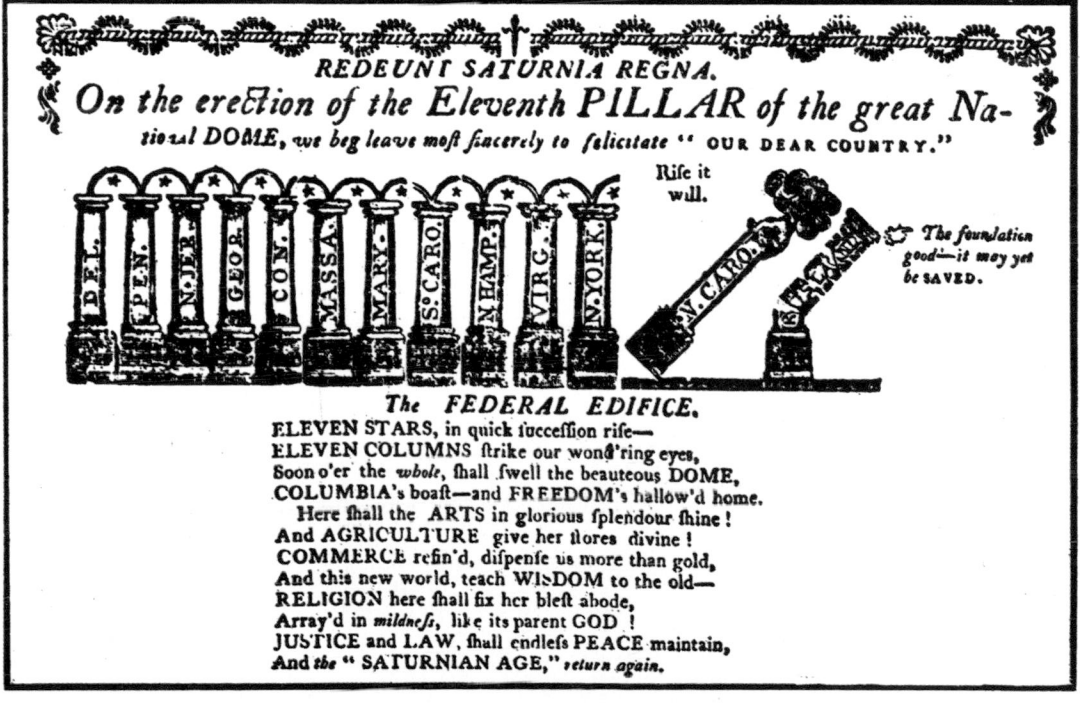

This political cartoon about ratifying the Constitution appeared in the newspaper the *Massachusetts Sentinel* in 1788.

Travels of the Constitution

The day after the four-page Constitution was signed, the document was put on a stagecoach headed for New York and the U.S. Congress.

From 1789 to 1921, the Secretary of State took over the care of the document. During those years, the Constitution moved as often as the government did. For example, the papers were sent by ship to the new capital of Washington, D.C., in 1800.

The War of 1812 also threatened the Constitution's safety. So in 1814, the papers were stuffed into cloth bags and carted to Virginia. There the Constitution remained safe while the British burned the White House, Capitol, and other buildings. The Constitution was returned to the capital city in September that same year. The document continued to be moved from office to office. However, it was always wrapped and kept flat in a steel case.

On September 29, 1901, the Constitution was moved to the Library of Congress. This time it made the trip in a Model-T Ford mail wagon. It was cushioned on a pile of leather mail sacks. At the Library of Congress, the pages were kept in an office safe until ready for public display.

Congress spent $12,000 to develop a case to protect the document. The Constitution remained on display in its special case of marble, bronze, and glass until 1941. That is when the attack on Pearl Harbor occurred during World War II (1939–1945). The attack caused alarm, and the Constitution again was moved. This time its pages were put in a special bronze container sealed with lead. This container was packed into an oak box and sent by train to Fort Knox in Kentucky, where the country's gold is kept. The Constitution stayed in a vault there until September 1944, when it was returned to the Library of Congress.

The Constitution's last move came in December 1952 to the National Archives building. For this move, the papers rode on mattresses in a Marine Corps vehicle accompanied by motorcycles, guards, military bands, two tanks, and four military men carrying submachine guns. (See the photo at left.)

Only the first and last pages of the Constitution were displayed at the National Archives. But on September 15, 2000, the second page was added to the display. The pages are kept in a scientifically designed bulletproof case. Every night, this case is lowered into a large safe with 5-ton (5,080-kilogram) doors meant to survive a nuclear explosion.

All four pages of the Constitution are on display only one day a year. That day is September 17, Constitution Day, the anniversary of the document's signing.

Chapter Six

Amendments

Many of the states approved the Constitution with a certain understanding. They wanted specific rights and freedoms added to the document soon after its ratification. The new Congress met in 1789 to address this issue.

James Madison reviewed more than 100 different suggestions from the states. From these, Madison proposed 12 amendments, 10 of which Congress approved. These 10 amendments to the Constitution are known as the Bill of Rights. They became part of the Constitution in 1791.

How the Constitution Is Amended

Amendments begin as proposals. To become an amendment, a proposal must pass several approvals. It must have support from two-thirds of both the House of Representatives and the Senate. It also must have support from three-fourths of the states.

Congress of the United States
begun and held at the City of New-York, on
Wednesday the fourth of March, one thousand seven hundred and eighty nine.

THE

RESOLVED

ARTICLES

Article the first

Article the second

Article the third

Article the fourth

Article the fifth

Article the sixth

Article the seventh

Article the eighth

Article the ninth

Article the tenth

Article the eleventh

Article the twelfth

ATTEST,

Speaker of the House of Representatives.

John Adams, Vice President of the United States, and President of the Senate.

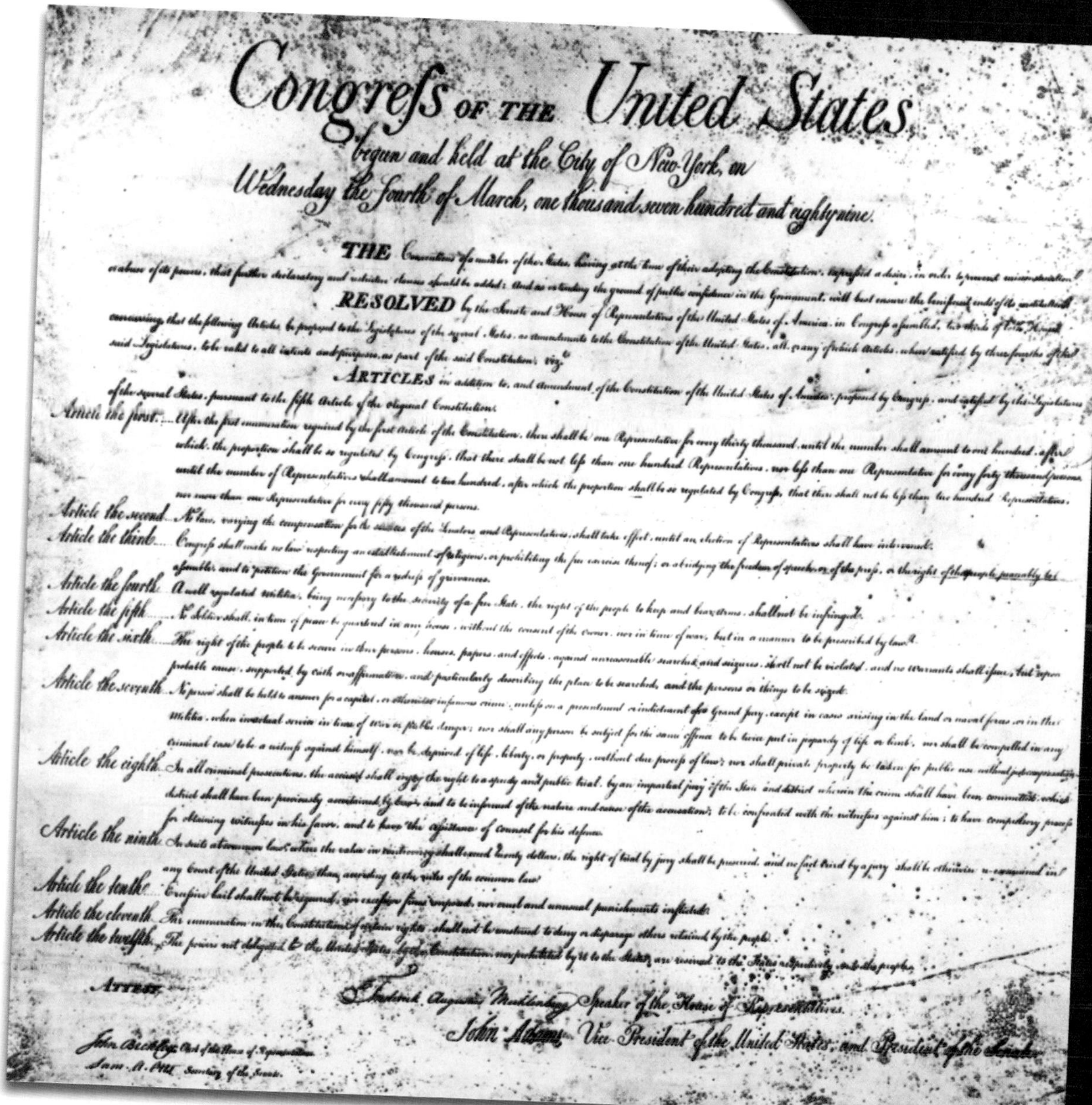

The first 10 amendments to the Constitution are called the Bill of Rights. Madison's original 12 proposals are shown above.

Another way amendments can be proposed is through a national convention called by Congress. Two-thirds of the state legislatures must request this convention. So far, this method has never been used.

More than 10,000 amendments have been suggested. However, the Constitution has been amended only 27 times.

Under the First Amendment, Americans have the right to assemble peacefully in public places.

A Summary of the Bill of Rights

The First Amendment: Provides Americans with freedom of speech, freedom of religion, and freedom of assembly

The Second Amendment: Gives people the right to keep and bear arms (guns and other weapons)

The Third Amendment: Keeps homeowners from having to let soldiers stay in their homes; This amendment was included because of events during the Revolutionary War when Britain forced Americans to take in soldiers.

The Fourth Amendment: Protects people from having their homes unlawfully searched

The Fifth Amendment: Outlines steps that must be taken if someone is charged with a crime

The Sixth Amendment: Guarantees fair and speedy trials for people who are charged with crimes

The Seventh Amendment: Covers civil lawsuits that involve private rights; Such cases may be brought to a jury trial if they involve a sum of $20 or more.

The Eighth Amendment: Protects people who commit a crime from cruel and unusual punishment

The Ninth Amendment: Guarantees rights that may not be mentioned in the Bill of Rights

The Tenth Amendment: Limits the federal government by saying that powers not given to the federal government under the Constitution belong to the states and the people

Amendments That Never Made It

Here are examples of some suggested amendments that failed and the years they were proposed.

1876: Get rid of the United States Senate

1893: Rename the nation "United States of the Earth"

1914: Make divorce illegal

1933: Limit each person's wealth to $1 million

The Constitution Today

In colonial times, people did not think a large country could be run without a king. But the founding fathers created a document that lasted and a form of government that worked. Although the 4,400-word Constitution is the shortest constitution of any national government, it has stayed in effect longer than any constitution in history.

Today, the Constitution not only guides the United States but also inspires other nations. Other countries have used it as a model when forming their own governments.

CONGRESS OF THE UNITED STATES.

In the House of Representatives,

Monday, 24th August, 1789,

RESOLVED, BY THE SENATE AND HOUSE OF REPRESENTA-
TIVES OF THE UNITED STATES OF AMERICA IN CONGRESS
ASSEMBLED, two thirds of both Houses deeming it necessary, That
the following Articles be proposed to the Legislatures of the several
States, as Amendments to the Constitution of the United States, all
or any of which Articles, when ratified by three fourths of the said
Legislatures, to be valid to all intents and purposes as part of the
said Constitution—Viz.

ARTICLES in addition to, and amendment of, the Constitution of
the United States of America, proposed by Congress, and ratified
by the Legislatures of the several States, pursuant to the fifth Article of the original Constitution.

ARTICLE THE FIRST.

After the first enumeration, required by the first Article of the
Constitution, there shall be one Representative for every thirty thousand, until the number shall amount to one hundred, after which
the proportion shall be so regulated by Congress, that there shall
be not less than one hundred Representatives, nor less than one Representative for every forty thousand persons, until the number of
Representatives shall amount to two hundred, after which the proportion shall be so regulated by Congress, that there shall not be less
than two hundred Representatives, nor less than one Representative
for every fifty thousand persons.

ARTICLE THE SECOND.

No law varying the compensation to the members of Congress,
shall take effect, until an election of Representatives shall have in-
tervened.

ARTICLE THE THIRD.

Congress shall make no law establishing religion or prohibiting
the free exercise thereof, nor shall the rights of Conscience be infringed.

ARTICLE THE FOURTH.

The freedom of Speech, and of the Press, and the right of the
People peaceably to assemble, and to apply to the Government for a redress of grievances, shall
not be infringed.

This photo shows a working copy of the Bill of Rights, an important
additon to the U.S. Constitution.

TIMELINE

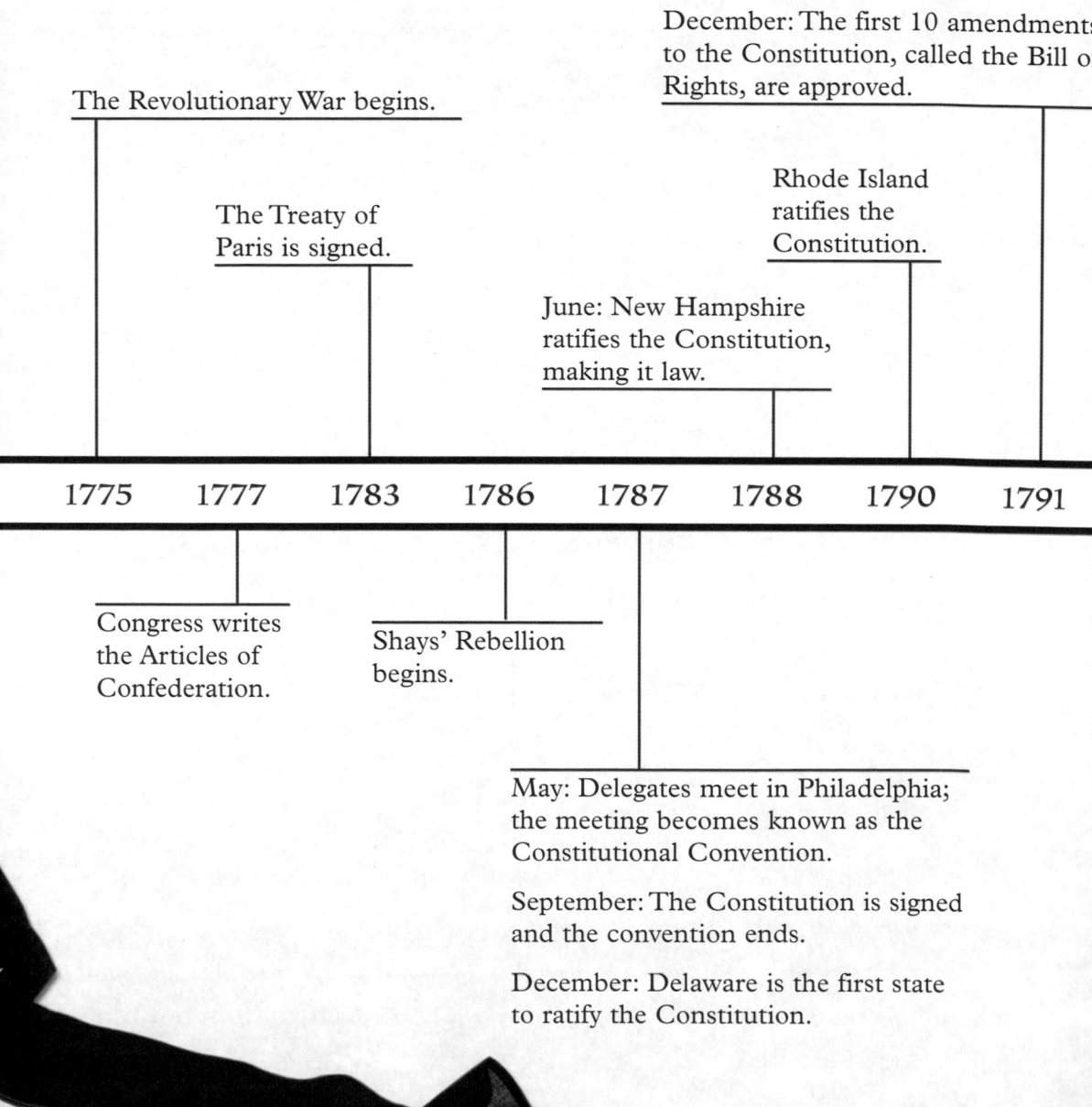

The Revolutionary War begins.

December: The first 10 amendments to the Constitution, called the Bill of Rights, are approved.

The Treaty of Paris is signed.

Rhode Island ratifies the Constitution.

June: New Hampshire ratifies the Constitution, making it law.

| 1775 | 1777 | 1783 | 1786 | 1787 | 1788 | 1790 | 1791 |

Congress writes the Articles of Confederation.

Shays' Rebellion begins.

May: Delegates meet in Philadelphia; the meeting becomes known as the Constitutional Convention.

September: The Constitution is signed and the convention ends.

December: Delaware is the first state to ratify the Constitution.

THIRTIETH CONGRESS—FIRST SESSION.

S. 31.

IN THE HOUSE OF REPRESENTATIVES.

JANUARY 12, 1848.

Read twice, and committed to a Committee of the Whole House to-morrow.

AN ACT

To provide for the purchase of the manuscript papers of the late James Madison, former President of the United States.

1   Be it enacted by the Senate and House of Repre-
2 sentatives of the United States of America in Congress
3 assembled, That the sum of twenty-five thousand dollars
4 be, and the same is hereby, appropriated out of any money
5 in the treasury, not otherwise appropriated, to purchase of
6 Mrs. D. P. Madison, widow of the late James Madison,
7 formerly President of the United States, all the unpublish-
8 ed manuscript papers of the said James Madison now
9 belonging to and in her possession, and upon delivery
10 thereof to the Secretary of State, with a proper convey-
11 ance of title to the United States, the said sum of money,
12 upon the certificate of the Secretary of State of the de-
13 livery and conveyance of said papers, shall be paid at the
14 treasury, agreeably to the wishes of the said Mrs. Madi-
15 son, and in the manner following, namely, five thousand

43

Glossary

amend (uh-MEND)—to change something; an amendment to the Constitution makes a change to it.

compromise (KOM-pruh-mize)—a settlement of differences in which each side gives up some of its demands

constitution (kon-stuh-TOO-shuhn)—a written document containing the basic principles of a government

convention (kuhn-VEN-shuhn)—a large gathering of people who have the same interests

delegate (DEL-uh-guht)—a person chosen to represent other people at a meeting

override (oh-vur-RIDE)—to reject or not accept something

protest (PROH-test)—a demonstration against something

ratify (RAT-uh-fye)—to approve officially

revolution (rev-uh-LOO-shuhn)—the fight to replace a system of government; in the American Revolution, colonists fought against Britain and formed a new government.

treaty (TREE-tee)—a formal agreement between two or more countries

veto (VEE-toh)—to stop a bill from becoming law; the president can veto a bill presented by Congress.

For Further Reading

Collier, Christopher, and James Lincoln Collier. *Creating the Constitution: 1787.* The Drama of American History. New York: Benchmark Books, 1999.

Hakim, Joy. *From Colonies to Country.* History of US. New York: Oxford University Press, 1999.

Kelley, Brent. *James Madison: Father of the Constitution.* Revolutionary War Leaders. Philadelphia: Chelsea House Publishers, 2001.

Perrin, Pat, and Wim Coleman, eds. *The Constitution and the Bill of Rights.* Researching American History. Carlisle, Mass.: Discovery Enterprises, 2000.

Weber, Michael. *The Young Republic.* Making of America. Austin, Tex.: Raintree Steck-Vaughn, 2000.

Places of Interest

Colonial Williamsburg
Southeast Virginia, midway
between Richmond and Norfolk
on I-64
Allows visitors to experience what
life was like in colonial times

**Independence National
Historical Park**
Third and Chestnut Streets
Philadelphia, PA 19106
Includes Independence Hall,
where the Constitutional
Convention took place

The James Madison Museum
129 Caroline Street
Orange, VA 22960-1532
First museum dedicated to the
father of the Constitution and
fourth president of the
United States

**National Archives and
Records Administration**
700 Pennsylvania Avenue NW
Washington, DC 20408
The Constitution is kept on
display here.